Virtual worlds are
emotional outlets

Best

Myers

July 07

Virtual Worlds™

Rewiring
Your Emotional
Future

Jack Myers
With Jerry Weinstein

Myers Publishing, LLC
125 W. 80th Street
New York, NY 10024
jm@jackmyers.com
www.jackmyers.com
212-875-8004

Library of Congress Control No: 2007901546

First printing : April 2007
Printed in the United States of America.
Published simultaneously in Canada.

ISBN   978-0-9793887-1-2

FOREWORD

Virtual Worlds: Rewiring Your Emotional Future:
A Radically New Reader Generated Book Publishing Concept

Virtual Worlds:™ *Rewiring Your Emotional Future* by Jack Myers with Jerry Weinstein is a radically different type of book that both discusses the explosive impact that the proliferation of Virtual Worlds is having on culture, society and business today, and also invites readers themselves to actually become contributors to the book, even sharing in future revenues and rights deals.

Virtual Worlds and enhanced social networks allow people to explore and experience new universes, while expanding their emotional range and depth, changing the nature of communication, and creating different identities. Since virtual worlds and social networks are just beginning to emerge as a major force in society, veteran media and cultural visionary Jack Myers shares insights on how this new Internet development will impact society and relationships and alter the emotional DNA of future generations. *Virtual Worlds: Rewiring Your Emotional Future* is a completely new type of book. For your $15.95 you have purchased not only this 122-page volume but you can also register to receive regular quarterly updates on Virtual Worlds, including Jack Myers' recommendations, insights and observations plus interviews with key figures in the virtual world landscape. Plus Myers is offering readers the chance to become part of the book themselves by sharing their own virtual world experiences and having them included in the quarterly updates. Visit www.jackmyers.com for information.

Virtual Worlds: Rewiring Your Emotional Future also introduces the first chapter of a new "reader generated" novel: *CyberParadiseSociety.com*, taking readers 25-years into the future when a leading virtual world has such an enormous impact on society that it can radically alter politics, entertainment, and interpersonal relationships. Myers introduces an unfolding drama within the corporate parent of the CyberParadiseSociety virtual world, Global Paradise Games, that threatens not only the company but the millions of CyberParadiseSociety "residents." This very first "reader generated book" invites readers to submit their ideas for the next chapter, which Myers will select and publish, followed by reader submissions for each future chapter. Every writer whose chapter is selected will gain rights for participation in any future revenues for movie rights, game rights etc. Visit www.jackmyers.com for information.

A growing number of young people are spending unprecedented amounts of time in a virtual existence.

Virtual Worlds are becoming an embedded part of our culture and the implications for every aspect of society are unimaginable. This 116-page easy-to-read book discusses the potential that Virtual Worlds have to dramatically alter the emotional code of the human race, and also reviews the opportunities for individuals, corporations, advertising and media companies to build personal and corporate marketing campaigns in Virtual Worlds. This first reader generated book not only will open the eyes of readers to this completely new world but, in itself, will become an immersive experience for readers that could keep them involved, engaged and emotionally connected to a virtual world community experience for years ahead.

TABLE OF CONTENTS

The Internet as we know it today is an amoebic form of a new universe that is just beginning to be explored and developed. There is an endless quest ahead that will be very real and fascinating.

CHAPTER 1

TAKING YOUR FIRST BREATH
IN A VIRTUAL WORLD

Virtual Worlds™ are 21st Century versions of 1960s mind-expanding drugs, but they are expanding more than just the mind. Virtual worlds and enhanced social networks allow us to explore new universes, expand our emotional range and depth, change the nature of communication and create different identities for ourselves. You can now create multiple versions of yourself with different names, gender, ethnic heritage, passions, dreams and even relationships.

Traditional identities and communities have defined civilization for centuries, but in the 21st Century a new world has opened that is radically altering how we define ourselves and how others perceive us. Second Life, Neopets, there.com, Sims, Cyworld, Kaneva, Doppelganger, MySpace, Friendster, TagWorld, Facebook, Gaia, hi5, Multiply and hundreds of new communities are being built in a completely new universe. Second Life is the first great city built in this new world, a bustling chaotic uncontrolled gathering place, like Chicago in the 19th century.

In a virtual community, you can create a new identity or extend the one you live every day in the traditional world. You can test drive new personalities, changing or even completely discarding them if they don't reflect who you *want* to be. I can create new models of Jack Myers like BMW releases new model cars. I can be the author of this book in the physical world and create multiple parallel lives in completely new virtual worlds.

Avatars are computer images that can be human, animal or anything the imagination can conjure. You design the color, the language, the hairstyle, and the fashion right down to the underwear. Avatars are computerized Barbie and Ken dolls on steroids, self-centered with all their favorite things around them. The creator personalizes his or her avatar with an endless list of available options offered in the virtual world. Of course, they come with a cost, which you pay with currency acquired by successfully "living" in the cyber universe.

In online communities, dating sites and social networks you can be whoever you choose to be. You can create and "live" completely separate and distinct profiles. You can live in New York, Peoria, Hollywood or Seoul; on a college campus, alone or with your family. You can enter virtual communities whenever you want, turning them on and off like a TV.

Psychologists report a child's virtual self often reflects more about their core self-image than the self they display in their day-to-day behavior. Their virtual selves display their feelings about authority, their likes and dislikes unfettered by parental influence and controls. The worlds in which they immerse themselves often reflect more about their self-identities and how they want to be perceived than their more traditional activities and choices.

The 19-year old PS3 gamer who drives more miles on virtual highways and racecourses every week than on pavement and asphalt sees each of these worlds from a very different perspective. The worlds he watches from the windows of both his virtual and mechanical cars both change daily, with new billboards, buildings under construction and seasonal changes. He's engaged intellectually, stimulated emotionally and physically activated in ways that are not even closely comparable. Which world is most *real* to him: traditional or virtual? Where is he more comfortable and at home? In the virtual world or on a highway and congested city streets? Which world is more inviting, appealing and conducive to forming lifelong behavior patterns?

Entering a virtual world is the equivalent of an amphibian taking its first tentative steps out of water and discovering how to breathe. To the amphibian, is one world real and the other not? Is a virtual existence in Second Life or gaming sites any less "real" than time spent at a friend's home?

Most of us are more comfortable in the *physical* traditional world than in virtual worlds, but a growing number of young people are spending unprecedented amounts of time in a virtual existence. According to a new Myers media usage study, 72 percent of 18 to 24 year olds spend more than an hour daily online for fun and 38 percent spend more than an hour daily playing videogames. Significant and steadily increasing amounts of time are being committed to e-mail, instant messaging and text messaging. These activities, now mostly requiring separate technologies and programs, are being merged into one cross-platform all-engaging and completely immersive experience within the new Virtual Worlds that will soon be as ubiquitous as

MySpace and YouTube.

Is it more or less "natural" to create an avatar for social networking in the *Second Life* Virtual World than starting school in a new city? Is life in a Virtual World perceived as less relevant than time spent at school, at a job or watching TV at home? Scientists, sociologists and anthropologists suggest that active social participation and involvement in online virtual worlds is a more constructive and healthy human experience than passively watching television, reading a book, or being in an unhappy job or relationship. In the next several decades, we'll find out if they are right.

Virtual worlds are becoming an embedded part of our culture and the implications for every aspect of society are unimaginable. When you enter a Virtual World you are stepping into space, into a new universe with no preparation, no training, no experience and no knowledge of what the future will bring or how it will impact you.

The Internet as we know it today is an amoebic form of a new universe that is just beginning to be explored and developed. There is an endless quest ahead that will be very real and fascinating. The Internet is opening a new world that will manifest in myriad forms, from the most simple search engines to complex and immersive virtual communities. New sites, formats and amazingly complex and absorbing cyber civilizations are on the horizon. They have the potential to radically alter the emotional code of the human race.

www.SecondLife.com // Avatar flying to a power plant

www.SecondLife.com // Avatars in Ideas City

www.SecondLife.com // Happy avatar couple

www.SecondLife.com // Avatars chatting at the bar on the beach

How many times have you said "I feel it in my gut" or "I'm heartsick?" The only thing we typically *feel* in our brain is a headache.

CHAPTER 2

INTERNET ALTERS HOW WE PERCEIVE MESSAGES MORE THAN HOW WE RECEIVE THEM

The Internet offers extraordinary opportunities to literally recreate your life at every level — for better or for worse. It has already become an essential part of the lifestyle and work of a vast majority of Americans and people around the globe. Every aspect of life is being radically altered by the Internet. And we have experienced just the tip of the iceberg.

Surviving these changes — learning to breathe the new virtual air — will be easy, just as new media technologies have become second nature for most of us. As Wi-Fi Clouds and Ultra Wi-Fi become commonplace... as mobile devices become an elegant extension of the home video center... as wireless communications becomes the norm... as chips are literally embedded in our bodies so we no longer require bulky phones or iPods... as our brains learn to discern and process digital signals... as our bodies become our own personal energy sources... we will quickly adapt and wonder how we lived without these advances.

But there will also be changes that are not advanced through science, technology and research. They are the changes to how we emotionally perceive ourselves, how we build our place in the many worlds in which we will simultaneously exist, and how we respond to the evolution of virtual worlds and multiple selves.

Our emotional DNA is being rewired.

ADVERTISERS CATCH ONTO
REWIRING THE EMOTIONAL DNA

Leave it to advertisers to be first to catch onto changes in the human emotional DNA. Advertisers, who have relied almost exclusively on data and scientific research methodologies for decision-making for all of the 20th Century, are looking elsewhere to build new advertising models in the 21st Century. With all the resources available to them for defining and reaching the best target audiences, the most likely shoppers, the optimum spenders, they are looking elsewhere to develop their advertising strategies. In the next ten years, reliance on Nielsen ratings and other behavioral data will become marginalized as marketers learn to rely instead on new measures of performance based on a combination of return-on-investment and insights on consumer emotions, passions and feelings.

Advertisers are investing millions — and soon will be investing billions — to gain a better understanding of how *emotions* drive decisions and

21

what role emotions play in the products we buy, our loyalties, and the connections we make and break. The search for emotional connections inspired Sears Roebuck & Company to sponsor *Extreme Makeover: Home Edition*, Coca-Cola and AT&T to identify themselves with *American Idol*, Fox to acquire *MySpace* for $600 million, American Express to align with the Tribeca Film Festival, Axe deodorant to sponsor disruptive media events, Saatchi & Saatchi to align its future behind Kevin Roberts' *Lovemarks, and Esquire* magazine to build dream bachelor pads in New York and Los Angeles. Sears and other retailers are opening retail outlets in Second Life, joining entrepreneurs who have already settled in. Marketers and corporations are embedding themselves to explore these unexplored territories.

By focusing on emotional connections, advertisers are dramatically altering traditional creative and media strategies that have been sacrosanct in the ad business for decades. Of 3,000 television commercials reviewed in 2005 and 2006, more than 2,200 offered access to additional information through a toll free phone number or URL.

22

The core question for these marketers is what are the emotional dynamics that motivate consumers to react to one message and not another, and how the environment in which ad messages are presented impacts on these dynamics.

Consider the process of looking at an ad message or just reading this book. The words or messages enter through the eyes and progress instantly to the cerebral cortex, the part of the brain that controls intelligence, where they are processed and evaluated, activating any number of responses. Reading is an intuitive ability that we learned as children and that has become second nature. But messages — in all forms and from multiple sources — enter our experience through all our senses. We have been taught and believe they first travel to the brain, which then sends appropriate response signals to different nerve centers, organs, limbs and muscles.

In fact, scientists and psychiatrists are proving that as we read, see, smell, touch, hear and feel, messages are sent not just to the brain but simultaneously to two other emotional centers: our heart and gut. There is a small, prune-like part of the brain located under the frontal-lobes, called the insula, that is thought to register gut feelings and has recently been recognized as a critical part of a network that sustains addictive behavior such as smoking. Addicts, no matter how much they may want to change their addictive behavior, are "locked-in" by the insula. The brain has, in essence, captured dictatorial powers over emotional — and physical — well-being. As new generations learn in Virtual Worlds how to empower emotional centers to gain power and control equal to the brain, the natural evolutionary process will ultimately lead to a rebalancing of the human psyche, spirit and ego.

There are undoubtedly other emotional centers that human beings have not yet activated and that are waiting to come to life in Virtual Worlds. But we all recognize our heart and gut constantly compete with our brain. We process our emotional responses to sensory inputs separately and simultaneously in our heart and in our gut as well as in our brain. How many times have you said "I feel it in my gut" or "I'm heartsick?" The only thing we typically *feel* in our brain is a headache. It's a biological conflict to *think* about how we emotionally *feel.*

It's ironic, then, that we tend to deal with emotions by applying brainpower.

Why do we believe we need to sleep on decisions and allow our brains to process our feelings before we act on them?

Why do we seek mental clarity and spend billions and billions on psychiatrists and psychologists to get in touch with our feelings through our thought process, rather than finding new and better ways to listen to our hearts and guts?

When our brain conflicts with either our heart or gut, the brain wins out nine times out of ten for the average person. Impulse items are stocked near retail checkout lines to bypass intellectual considerations, but then we often regret those purchases when we take the time to think about them.

CHAPTER 3

BRAIN, HEART AND GUT :
THREE CENTRAL HUMAN OPERATING
SYSTEMS

Holistic and Oriental medicine practitioners listen and learn from the total self. They recognize the importance of evaluating hundreds of points in the body. They understand the multiple independent and interdependent energy networks that flow through the body, each with its own powerful central operating system centered in the brain *and* the heart and gut.

These operating systems function within us like separate governments that co-exist but also conflict. Within each operating system is a "treasury department" that manufactures currencies: in the brain the currency is **thoughts;** in the heart and gut, the currency is **emotions**. Thoughts and emotions are the gas that powers our engines, but in our culture and society we have learned to repress our emotions and not trust our feelings. To be fair, we're also often advised to "keep our thoughts to ourselves," but few of us actually follow that advice.

When our brain conflicts with either our heart or gut, the brain wins out nine times out of ten for the average person. Impulse items are stocked near retail checkout lines to bypass intellectual considerations, but then we often regret those purchases when we take the time to think about them.

The inevitable end result of constantly repressing our emotions consciously and sub-consciously is that our poor heart and gut suffer from inferiority complexes.

When it comes to running and ruling the world as we experience it every day, the brain has become omnipotent. Of course, we make gut decisions and follow our hearts, but how often does an executive, government official, teacher, computer engineer or anyone else act on their gut instinct or heart's desire?

The conflict between emotions and intellect drive many of our greatest challenges. Warriors are spurred on with propaganda messages that target emotional commitments rather than intellectual. The legal system is designed to operate on facts but attorneys appeal to jurors with emotional arguments. Abortion, global warming, education... name an issue and at the core there's almost always the battle between the intellectual point-of-view and the emotional feelings the issue evokes.

Today, large governments manage decisions based on the collective brain power of their leaders. Revolutionary organizations thrive on their emotional fervor. With one group, thinking overpowers their emotions; with the other, emotions direct their actions. Traditional western societies and cultures are brain-led, driven by mental rather than emotional decisions. Eastern cultures, and many revolutionary groups, typically have emotional influences at their foundation.

Corporations are brain-led and the larger corporations become, the more brain-led they are. Except for rare exceptions, like News Corp and its gut-led leader Rupert Murdoch, companies are required to operate almost exclusively on brain-based management.

I've been studying corporate America for 25 years focusing on television, entertainment, marketing, media and advertising. In that quarter-century, I've become known for the accuracy of my forecasts and I've made more than 5,000 of them. I'm going to admit something that will probably harm the credibility of my future forecasts, but the primary tool I use to develop my predictions is not data and information; it's my gut instinct.

Yes, I gather extensive input and data. But unlike every other leading economic forecaster in the media and advertising business, I don't depend on that data to draw my conclusions. Numerous times over the past 25 years, I've overruled what the facts say and what my brain tells me and go with my gut. Usually my brains and my gut agree, but when they don't, I've learned to trust my gut. Most successful companies in any creative field like entertainment and fashion have been built on the gut instinct and heartfelt beliefs of their founders. As companies grow, they become increasingly dependent on intellectually-based programs and policies that guide brain-led management, while the more emotionally grounded founders lose influence and control. Few positions within the average corporation permit management decisions that defy the facts and intelligence and instead are based on gut instinct and feelings. Thus the demise of Ted Turner once he merged his company into Time Warner.

Married couples shift from a relationship based on the emotions that led to their initial attraction to dealing with the day-to-day pressures, financial planning issues, home building, jobs, school, children's needs and brain-led values. Emotions suffer a loss of power and influence and they rebel, causing anger and depression. Anger is usually misplaced, targeted at a spouse or at yourself. The solution is almost always to stop over-thinking the problems and get back in touch with your heart and gut. When you let them guide you to the solutions that feel best, the brain will quietly follow, depression will ebb and peace will follow.

This simplistic rule applies to almost every relationship we have in all parts of our lives. But we've lost the skills, sensitivity and commitment required to transform our decision-making and actions from brain-led to heart and gut-led. So we turn to religion, gurus, cult leaders, spiritual advisors, the latest *Idiot's Guide*, celebrities, sports stars and faux guides to provide us with the emotional center we're unable to find within ourselves.

In Virtual Worlds we're bringing back to humanity the power and influence of the heart and gut. Online communities like MySpace, Facebook, YouTube, Second Life, Cyworld and even dating sites are huge successes because they empower emotions and offer a welcome environment where the heart and gut can thrive. Repressed and depressed emotions suddenly find joy and redemption. Online social networks and communities developed around shared beliefs and interests revive and stimulate the emotions. Virtual Worlds welcome us into a new society that devalues the intellectual stimuli and rewards emotional connections.

Today's social networks and virtual worlds are in their infancy. Virtual Worlds of the future will emulate life and foster relationships and interaction; and success in these worlds will be based on emotional rather than intellectual skills. For participants and marketers seeking to influence them, traditional brain-based methods and behaviors will be useless. But advertisers who have retained emotional connections as the foundation of their strategies will thrive.

www.SecondLife.com // Avatar audience for a virtual conference

www.SecondLife.com // Avatars relaxing in the sun

www.SecondLife.com // Avatars socializing and getting
ready for some virtual surf lessons

www.SecondLife.com // Avatars chatting about how
and where to earn linden dollars in Second Life

BusinessWeek's May 2006 cover story on Second Life was the tipping point. The article "fired up the corporate interest in SL as a marketing platform, and for better or worse, that also spurred on the mainstream media. Feedback loop from there, and now we're over a million."

CHAPTER 4

VIRTUAL WORLDS ARE
REAL TO RESIDENTS

While America broke the 300 million barrier in October 2006, online world Second Life hit a personal milestone of its own, its one-millionth registrant. By April 2007, residents numbered 4.7 million. Not bad given that the creation of *Linden Lab* was founded in 2003. Second Life is no mere online game. It's a "Metaverse" and the next generation of the Net. Its embrace will have volatile real world consequences in the realms of entertainment, commerce, and interpersonal relationships.

All of the talk about *Web 2.0* is seemingly trumped by online environments like There.com, activeworlds, and Second Life. SL is the 3-D Web. It is, as creator Phil Rosedale claims, a "full simulation of the world." Broadcaster Christopher Lyndon has referred to it as "the Louisiana Purchase of the mind." But just what is the magic and the mix that has attracted financial backing from Pierre Omidyar (eBay's founder) and Amazon's Jeff Bezos?

Wagner James Au has been an embedded journalist on SL since 2004. In an exclusive interview with *Jack Myers Media Business Report* he provided commentary on the online world's evolution, and insight into how it will profoundly impact life in the physical world.

BusinessWeek's May 2006 cover story on Second Life was the tipping point. The article "fired up the corporate interest in SL as a marketing platform, and for better or worse, that also spurred on the mainstream media. Feedback loop from there, and now we're over a million", says Au.

But who is "we"? Au points out "there's still quite a few new users coming into SL who are 'early adopter' in the fundamental understanding of the term - people who are comfortable with Second Life's fairly steep learning curve (certainly for high-level content creation like scripting and complex building). At the same time, they have even more casual social gamers who're just looking for a fun place to have parties and dance. So it's a strange and unique mix marrying 70 percent from the *AOL* demographic and 30 percent from the *Boing Boing/ Slashdot/Kotaku* demographic."

Asked to describe SL for different demographic groups, Au offers a trio of high concept pitches: "*Teen People*: it's a 3-D *MySpace*; *Conde Nast Traveler*: it's a world that looks like all the places described in this magazine. *AARP* is tougher: it's like the Web, except in 3-D computer animation like a *Pixar* movie that you get to be in, be whatever you want, and build whatever you like."

NOT YOUR FATHER'S VIDEOGAME

What distinguishes SL from other massively multiplayer (MMP) games is that while it takes advantages of the freedoms that gaming provides (you can fly, even teleport), there are no objectives. It's all about creating new identities and lives online. Residents, as they are called, meet, work, fall in love. And yes, they transact business. What makes Second Life unique is that, six months after its launch, its founders permitted residents to retain their Intellectual Property. What they create is theirs. When one visits Second Life for the first time, there is only a small fee. You are provided with a basic "avatar" - a virtual extension of yourself that may mirror your actual physical self, an idealized version (you with a killer personal trainer and/or *Dr. 90210* on retainer), or an utter reinvention (in terms of gender, sexuality, age, even species). The fun begins with customization, or "modding" (for modification). On Second Life, while your behavior defines your being, you simultaneously fashion your identity from the outside in - purchasing skins, clothing, accessories, even a personality. Soon we'll start to see products that were born on Second Life migrate to the physical world.

Brands Start From Scratch

Since appearance counts on Second Life, its earliest entrepreneurs have found particular success in developing its Red Light District, complete with gambling and sex shops. After an upgrade enabled residents to stream their desktop music into their Second Life world, dance clubs opened throughout the burg. Naturally, entertainment is big in this world. *SonyBMG* built their *Media Island* and are hosting launch parties and lives chats. Ben Folds "appeared" in October 2006 and other well-known singers and groups are performing regularly in Second life as the residents' avatars sit in the audience and watch/listen.

While Sony is on the right track with Media Island, Au cautions that it has many rivers to cross. "At the moment, a big brand like Sony will get you a nice thirty-minute diversion." Residents will show up, take a look at the content, and unless it's truly powerful, engaging and built to last, they'll leave to find the next diversion. It's not that the corporate content is of questionable quality, "it's just that residents churn through content so quickly, and unless there's a real sense of ongoing interactivity, they quickly get the idea in 15 to 30 minutes, and move on. Why hang out in an empty Sony kiosk when you can have a freeform build session in the sandbox with your friends?"

WELCOME TO THE NEW FRONTIER, FOLKS.

While eBay'ers and videogame players can "purchase reputations," it's the other way around on Second Life, Au suggests. "Proven creativity purchases reputation. Even real life celebrity only gets you so far. A new user comes in, and within the space of a few weeks, they're the talk of Second Life's veteran user base. And time and again, it's because they've created some truly unique content, or in some cases, a truly unique persona." Au points to a British resident named Robbie Dingo, who very shortly after joining SL earlier this year, had created a) virtual music instruments that actually work, b) a cool and somewhat dark game of Russian Roulette,

c) truly moving machinima and d) artificial marijuana plants that respond to sunlight and water, all of which caused a massive stir. "He's famous and part of that Second Life elite by sheer creative force," Au adds. Dingo's success was built on his ability to make emotional connections with other residents.

In this Virtual World, the traditional corporate model is at a disadvantage. As Au notes, they "only have money. I suppose if they really want to they could dedicate a staff to competing, but then, they're really at a disadvantage to a young mother on a farm with enormous talent and willingness to create a name for herself, and for whom even making $30,000 would be considered success." The platform itself is the equalizer.

Just as companies expand internationally and view China as a huge potential growth market, they will view Second Life and other immersive virtual worlds as new regions ripe for expansion.

CHAPTER 5

SAME PRINCIPLES APPLY TO VIRTUAL WORLD EXPANSION AS TO CHINA & OTHER NEW MARKETS

Much of the recent coverage on Virtual Worlds boils down to "trust me, it's the next big thing." But anyone who toiled, much less invested, in the dot com industry during the late nineties might rightfully shrink from such hype.

Today's burgeoning virtual worlds were gestating during the dot com boom of the late nineties. The earliest incarnations of virtual worlds were backed by some of today's media giants: Sony games have since fizzled, owing to the almost monolithic market share of *World of Warcraft*.) Back in 2001, economist Prof. Ed Castronova wrote *Virtual Worlds: A First-Hand Account of Market and Society on the Cyberian Frontier*. Early versions of virtual worlds were technologically unsophisticated, their business models were untested and unproven, and dot coms aplenty were filing for bankruptcy. Yet, Castronova was prescient to note that online worlds were taking off. His academic paper not only provides a template and back-story for virtual worlds, but it predicted that by 2006 virtual worlds would become a primary venue of online activity. Even if that estimate was just a bit premature, studies in South Korea, where *Cyworld* is a dominant pastime for millions, have recently shown that audiences prefer virtual worlds to television.

While Linden Labs' Phil Rosedale based Second Life on Neil Stephenson's novel *Snow Crash*, it was J.R.R. Tolkien who first coined "Secondary World" to describe his approach to literature. Players have participated in massively multiplayer online role-playing games, or MMORPGs since the early 1980's.

But it wasn't until 2002, with the launch of *The Sims Online*, that there was a game not based on killing. While the *Sims* was a failure in relation to expectations, it did prep users for Second Life, which to this day remains the most widely adopted non-genre 3D virtual world.

Author Wagner James Au believes that three factors account for SL's success:

1- User-created content;

2- A policy in which intellectual property rights to user-created content are retained by the creator;

3- An internal economy through which content creators could make some or all of their living from this creativity.

Even though role-playing is still central to communities such as *World of Warcraft* and *Entropia*, *Sims* and now *Second Life* push virtual worlds into a space that is neither fantasy nor reality. As Castronova defines them, fantasy is an invention of the mind; reality is subject to impositions of nature (such as scarcity and physics). Virtual worlds demand that we re-define our concept of reality itself.

The economic challenge is to define the growth potential of different virtual world formats. For example, *Second Life* requires a high learning curve and expertise in scripting, while MTV's *Virtual Laguna Beach* is essentially plug and play. While each offers a subscription model, Second Life's economy has taken what was deemed a $1 Billion economy in virtual world accessories and blown that number up, figuratively and financially.

Castronova's colleague at the University of Indiana, Professor Joshua Fairfield, his collaborator on numerous projects and papers, told *Jack Myers Media Business Report* that demand will support the growth of several virtual world business models. For example, Fairfield is confident that virtual entrepreneurs will include not only physical-world fashion designers but also programmers well-versed in scripting who will "trick out" your avatar. In fact, one such Second Life resident has arisen. Christiano Diaz, aka Christiano Midnight, has built a handful of businesses including *ANOmations*, which creates physical-world animations, and *Snapzilla*, which stores snapshots of residents (think *Flickr*) for Second Lifers.

According to Prof. Fairfield, virtual world economics will be impacted by the search-based economy that is prevalent today, with consumers differentiated based on how deeply they are prepared to invest in the search process to satisfy their needs. Taking a page from Barry Schwartz's *Paradox of Choice*, consumers are either "maximizers" or "suficers:" they either accept the first few search results even though they may not fully satisfy their needs, or they may drill down more deeply into the search process to find precisely what they want.

This experience has its analogue across our economy, and even resonates within virtual worlds. The amount of time we are willing to invest to immerse ourselves in a completely new economic, social and psychic universe determines our choice of virtual world experience. Experiences such as *Second Life* require deep immersion to achieve high satisfaction, while other "virtual world lite" experiences offer more play and are less likely to deliver the deep emotional satisfaction participants derive from fully immersive virtual worlds. What separates *Second Life* and *Cyworld* from emerging rivals is that residents of these worlds get to create virtual lives, complete with fully fledged economies and social relationships.

Fairfield speculates that the long-term economic success of Second Life depends on whether it can realize its business model of being an "operating system" where residents live, work and socialize. Fairfield suggests that social software might be created and deployed within virtual worlds to empower collaboration. Ultimately, these worlds become expansion opportunities for traditional "physical world" marketers. Just as companies expand internationally and view China as a huge potential growth market, they will view Second Life and other immersive virtual worlds as new regions ripe for expansion. And, in the same context, virtual world entrepreneurs will inevitably be first to market, opening retail outlets, developing service businesses and deploying marketing schemes. Already, buoyed that Second Life dollars (the Linden) trade $250 to $1 U.S., real estate developers are buying up both residential and commercial land for future sale.

In June 2006, Second Life hosted an avatar-based marketing panel in response to a series of articles in the *Harvard Business Review* on virtual worlds. SL residents were outspoken about their relationship to the marketplace. The gist seemed to be "Don't sell to me; engage with me." Unlike consumers in the physical world who have become de-sensitized to marketing, *Second Lifers* seem to cue into every new addition to their metaverse. SL has evolved in ways analogous to Cambridge's Harvard Square, which has zoned out fast food for decades. The same vigilance and control is being applied by Second Life residents.

While marketers have an easy path to adapt videogames and "virtual world lite" entries to their traditional marketing techniques, the immersive virtual world experiences will be more difficult to crack. Advertisers seeking an easy path to expose consumers to their messages will experience the same low level of satisfaction they now derive from most ad investments. It will suffice, but not satisfy.

Marketers who pursue a "maximizer" philosophy will need to approach virtual worlds in the same model they approach expansion to any new geographic market, such as China or Latin America. They will require specialists knowledgeable about the virtual world market; they will require marketing research that focuses on emotional connections more than exposure and recall; they will need "inside" partners and employees. Finally, they will need to make long-term investments with the understanding that the competition will be commensurate with how early-to-market they are, how long they are willing to invest before they will see their first dollar return on investment, and how emotionally relevant they are to residents.

For more information, link to www.Terranova.com, a collaborative Weblog launched by Edward Castronova and Julian Dibbell. It includes postings by Joshua Fairfield and Unggi Yoon, an expert on the South Korean market. Castronova published *Synthetic Worlds: The Business and Culture of Online Games* in 2005; it is now available in paperback.

www.SecondLife.com // Avatar audience for sport event

www.SecondLife.com // GSD&M avatars conference around the flying board room touring Idea City

www.SecondLife.com // Avatars in Reuters News Room

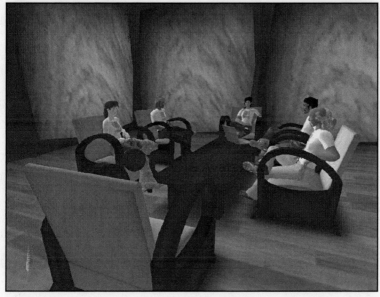

www.SecondLife.com // NMC Avatars in a corporate meeting

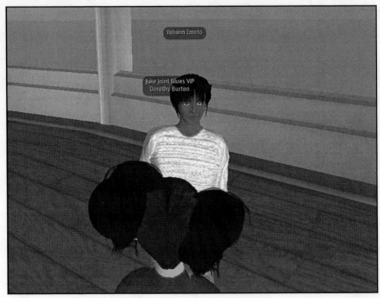

www.SecondLife.com // Avatars flirting

www.SecondLife.com // Avatars at a campfire

www.Gaiaonline.com // Avatars

www.Gaiaonline.com // Avatars playing online games

www.There.com // Avatar in mushroom land

www.There.com // Avatars in a party

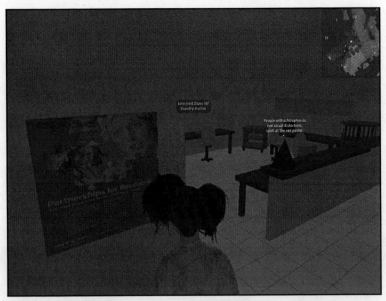

www.SecondLife.com // Poster reads:
Partnership for Recovery

www.SecondLife.com // Altered by schizophrenia poster
reads: Partner**shit face**recovery

The University of California at Davis created Virtual Hallucinations to give people the experience of having schizophrenia, enabling loved ones to have an appreciation of the experience those suffering are going through.

CHAPTER 6

AD AGENCIES AND CORPORATIONS EMBRACE SECOND LIFE EXPANSION

AGENCIES PITCHING NEW BUSINESS IN SECOND LIFE

Sears Roebuck & Company recently announced it would be opening its first store on *Second Life*. Ad agencies Leo Burnett, Crayon, GSD&M and several others have opened their offices on Second Life and are encouraging their clients to do the same. Several auto manufacturers, apparel companies, retailers and others are actively engaged in Second Life already or exploring opportunities.

Austin-based ad agency GSD&M has launched a lecture series at its elaborate Second Life headquarters, known as Idea City. GSD&M senior planner Joel Greenberg (Second Life name Kweisi Mfune), who suggested the development of Idea City in 2004, says he sometimes "feels like the guy who's explaining rock 'n roll to parents in 1965."

"In a world where knowledge wants to be free, how do marketers understand the implications and respond," Greenberg asked in an exclusive interview with *Jack Myers Media Business Report*. "Marketers are overwhelmed by the rate of technological change. If they understand the trends, when change comes they can at least anticipate their implications conceptually." GSD&M is a founding member of the MIT Convergence Culture Consortium www.convergenceculture.net) along with Turner Broadcasting, MTV Networks and Yahoo!. At Second Life, GSD&M has launched a lecture series discussing Internet trends, 'connectivity' in advertising, and other emerging issues. At Idea City, the GSD&M office features a massive virtual circular conference table where avatars of clients and guests can sit and take a tour of Second Life as the table literally takes off and flies around the virtual world.

Greenberg says GSD&M established a presence at Second Life because "a lot of our clients are targeting the creative class and a lot of people in Second Life are creative types of folks. It's a very interesting place to learn about innovation and how to behave differently as marketers. It's a good place to learn about community and how to market to communities. What we learn about communities on Second Life can be applied to communities in the physical world." GSD&M clients involved in Second Life include BMW, Chili's and Southwest Airlines.

"It's all about participation and engagement, not about advertising," says Greenberg.

"We are developing plans for research on Second Life to understand who the people are who are participating and what the relationship is between virtual experiences and physical world purchase behavior. We hope to work with 'in world' brands to help them reach more people in Second

Life." The concept that an ad agency in Second Life can attract clients that exist only in the virtual world is a radical one. Greenberg mentions potential clients like *Abbots Aerodrome,* an inworld airport where you can buy flying machines and learn to virtual sky dive.

Greenberg also says he hopes to do pro bono work for inworld brands, pointing out many communities in Second Life are for mutual support. The University of California at Davis created *Virtual Hallucinations* to give people the experience of having schizophrenia, enabling loved ones to have an appreciation of the experience those suffering are going through.

"Second Life gives us the ability to connect with people in ways we have never even been able to imagine and allows people to participate in a wide variety of groups they never had access to before. He mentions the teen age daughter of a friend who uses Xbox Live and plays with kids in Scotland, considering them a peer group of friends. "She talks with them on Skype while they're playing, knows Scottish slang, and has a sense of what it's like to grow up in another country and participate in social groups with people around the world."

Greenberg acknowledges Second Life needs better collaboration tools before the business takes off. He says Linden Labs is talking about open sourcing the client software and is working to clean up the code and add other programming languages. He believes 3D worlds will proliferate as technology enables improved communications tools. "But development is ultimately about people, not technology," he emphasizes. "Joining a virtual world is a lot like going to a new high school. At first it seems weird but once you fall into a group that shares your interests you understand the fun. Other people keep you inworld and until you meet other people you don't really have a reason to stay."

Greenberg recommends that first time Second Life residents spend an hour in *Orientation Island* to learn navigation and to visit www.slquery.com to "help find stuff that's interesting to you." He points out "Second Life is a beginning medium and the tools are not as mature as we would expect them to be coming from a Google world." There are regular events posted at Second Life, including concerts discussions, promotions and offerings.

Live music is especially popular in Second Life at the *Lily Pad Lounge*, *Muse Isle* and other clubs. Singers' avatars perform while the singer is in front of a computer microphone, with the music streamed live into a server. Typically there's interaction between the performer and audience.

"Communicating and marketing in Second Life is harder than making a media buy," says Greenberg. "In media you only need money and there's a fifty year tradition of how to buy an audience. Marketing like this is far more difficult; how do you involve people in Second Life and give them a positive experience?"

www.SecondLife.com // Sony BMG's entertainment center in Second Life

www.SecondLife.com // Susan Vega's avatar performing live music on stage, in front of an audience

MTVN's virtual franchise is MusicWorld, which promises to truly leverage MTV's core competency.

CHAPTER 7

VIRTUAL MTV: COMPLETELY REINVENTING THE MUSIC SCENE

Back in August 1981, The Buggles welcomed in the MTV era with the synth strings of their sardonic *Video Killed the Radio Star.* In a New York Minute music videos became the *lingua franca* of the recording industry. Flash forward to 2007: "residents" within *MTV Networks' MusicWorld* gather in an in-world club, their avatars blinged out in their Saturday night best to watch *Sucker Free,* belly up to the bar, and catch a few...videos.

Will virtual worlds kill the broadcast star, revitalize the video star, or both?

Until now, the build-out of virtual worlds has been the purview of software and game developers, and more recently, aggressive global telecoms. Certainly, a few media properties including BBC, Reuters, NPR, even SONY, are dipping their toes into Second Life, but MTV Networks was the first programmer to jump in with both feet and build from the ground up.

In an exclusive interview with *Jack Myers Media Business Report* Van Toffler, MTV Networks' Music/Logo/Film Group president, spoke about MTVN's ambitious undertaking.

The first of MTV Networks' worlds to launch was *Virtual Laguna Beach,* which had its soft launch in September 2006. While the minds behind VLB have clearly been influenced by Second Life, Toffler gave his staff marching orders to create the least intimidating user experience possible. His takeaway lesson from the success of the Internet: "Simple has won the day. Content creators need to rethink the process and unlearn their experience."

To achieve that end Virtual Laguna Beach developers have been advised by the founders of There.com and MIT's resident expert on convergence culture, Professor Henry Jenkins. Even their project name, *Leapfrog,* is a double-duty moniker. It is in essence a non-competitive children's game where everyone advances, while also echoing the military tactic of engaging the enemy while simultaneously advancing. Sun Tzu, anyone?

STRONG ENOUGH FOR A MAN
BUT MADE FOR A WOMAN

If one wanted to assess the economic potential of a virtual world, she'd be hard-pressed to find a better test tube than Laguna Beach, where shopping is what prayer is to the Bible Belt. While advertisers cottoned to an early VLB presentation, MTV is quick to indicate that this program is still in its infancy. Generating revenue is not its first priority, learning about the space is. That said, the demographic of the TV series has survived online intact: the ratio of women to men is 6:1, the median age is twenty. One can see why P&G's Secret and other advertisers targeting young females would want to lend their support as sponsors.

MTVN was savvy enough to create the perception of exclusivity within VLB. Recalling Google Mail's launch, only 100,000 invitations were offered to prospective charter VLB residents, nurturing a desire to get behind the virtual velvet rope. Since then it has seen an explosion of registrants as the community has grown 5,000 members a day with little publicity. At their own initiative residents have started 5,000 clubs and mounted their own prom in parallel to the show's event.

While Fox webcast the *The O.C.* season debut in MySpace, MTV outdid them by hosting a screening of the *Laguna Beach* season premiere *within* Virtual Laguna Beach. When the show's season wraps, VLB not only remains open, but continues to grow. In time guardians of VLB will have unprecedented access to community behavior via data that quantifies every action taken in-world: the number of times a user has altered their avatar, and what specific body part, what their retail experiences are like, their responses to entertainment streams. The phrase "vote with your feet" might be updated to "vote with your mouse-click."

UNPLUGGED GOES WIRELESS AND WI-FI

While shopping is an attribute of Laguna Beach and The Hills, music is after all the raison d'etre of MTV. While Urge Radio is the wallpaper within VLB, MTVN's virtual franchise is MusicWorld, which promises to truly leverage MTV's core competency. In 2006 *Wolfgang's Vault* opened the Concert Vault, an inventory of more than 300 full-length live concerts dating back to the Sixties. We're talking Sly and the Family Stone, The Cure, Bruce Springsteen, The Clash. Imagine experiencing these shows for the first time in a virtual world that replicates the physical music scene of the 1960s and 1970s, in some cases bringing classic musicians in-world to perform and chat about these gigs. Toffler views this space as a catalyst for "the complete reinvention of music."

LOGO AS A BLANK CANVAS

Perhaps most intriguing are MTV Networks' plans for **LogoWorld**. While the company has made three recent acquisitions, *AfterEllen, AfterElton,* and *365 Gay*, LogoWorld has been completely built bottom-up. While denizens of Virtual Laguna Beach can purchase a hooptie and a crib as part of a monthly subscription model, LogoWorld comes closer in pioneering spirit to Second Life. One can imagine that *House of Style's* Todd Oldham, star of Bravo's **Top Design,** will find his services in demand inworld.

Echoing the clarion call of his visionary peers, Toffler maintains that "media companies need to accept the notion of letting go." But will MTVN walk the walk? While adult content is a mainstay of Second Life, given the median age of VLB, that community is wisely pitched as PG-13. Feminists and fundamentalists alike who once railed at the sexual objectification of MTV's videos would find the space practically an abstinence-only public service announcement.

But in virtual worlds, brands are no longer under lock and key and will, to a greater extent, reflect what the audience wants. LogoWorld, for example, could become a leading force for the floor fight on Capitol Hill for hearings on "Don't Ask, Don't' Tell." Or, it could more closely mirror the consumerist underpinnings of Virtual Laguna Beach and be all about booking passage for *Rosie's R Family Vacation* cruise lines, gay adoption, and financial advice. Toffler suggests virtual worlds "add a layer of protection that is not there in MySpace or Facebook."

IMMERSION PAYS

While MTVN is soft-pedaling the revenue aspect of building virtual worlds around its media franchises, that doesn't mean that it hasn't modeled and quantified advertising costs for this emerging medium. While it's always gratifying to have a ratings behemoth be it Ozzie or Flava Flav, costs-per-thousand for video advertising delivered to highly targeted engaged residents of virtual worlds can reach $75 and beyond. "It's about another level of engagement," Toffler believes. MTVN tags the value of residents who put down roots inworld at $150 CPM, according to an industry expert, compared to average $20 CPMs for network television advertising and as low as $2 for standard online advertising. If this algorithm achieves proof of concept, you can bet that more media brands will be quickly acquiring virtual real estate.

Early data on Virtual Laguna Beach shows users spend quadruple the amount of time as they do on normal websites. Toffler believes virtual worlds will eventually extend to traditional media. "I hope there will be more content from virtual worlds that makes compelling TV," he says. MTVN is developing virtual experiments throughout the company and Toffler expects extensions of the company's brands to be developed across all platforms. "We want to leap into the next phase of 24/7 social networking with VOIP (voice over Internet protocol), Web 2.0, and virtual worlds."

www.SecondLife.com // Susan Vega's avatar during her onstage performance

www.SecondLife.com // Avatar audience for simulcast of a Susan Vegas' avatar live musical performance

It's not content that's at the core of new media; it's communications. Being connected to a network of friends is the killer app.

CHAPTER 8

WIRELESS IS THE NEXT FRONTIER

Being connected is what 16 to 32 years olds live for, says Sky Dayton, who founded EarthLink in 1994 at the age of 23 and is now CEO of Helio (a joint venture of EarthLink and SK Telecom). "It's not content that's at the core of new media; it's communications. Being connected to a network of friends is the killer app." In Korea, Dayton points out, mobile phones are being used for video conferences, Internet connectivity, and as a charge card for buying things. "They're downloading full-track music wherever they are, over the air. They're watching satellite TV beamed down to their handsets. And they're blogging like mad. When do people want to talk about life? It's when they're out living life; not when they happen to get back to their desktop computer." Dayton added, "Think about it. You're at a club or an art show and want to tell your friends about it. You're taking pictures and videos, and your device is location aware, and as you upload these images your device is GPS-tagging them, so if your friends are walking down the street at that moment, they can get an alert and come by. The new connections you can make between people are limitless. Do we want that experience here? Absolutely."

"Wireless," he added, "is the next frontier. It's the one device 16 to 32 year olds cannot live without and has a 24/7 connection with consumers that has entertainment companies salivating."

Dayton's advice is to realize "content will become particles of communication. Things will be discovered and shared, and what you discover and share will define who you are. You can't cut and paste the current model into this new medium. The linear flow of television," Dayton believes, "is done.

The unit of exchange in television is the show, not the network," which he referred to as "just a collection of shows with no brand identity."

"The unit of exchange in music today is the song," Dayton pointed out, "not the album." Nearly 900 million songs have been downloaded through iTunes; in the 4th quarter of 2006, 100 iPods were sold per minute and eight million iTunes videos were sold, Dayton pointed out.

Wall Street Journal columnist Walt Mossberg agrees the trends in digital entertainment are being led by wireless and e-commerce. He described Music Gremlin, a music player with Wi-Fi connectivity that will offer the ability to preview and download 1.7 million songs, and allow subscribers to "zap a song to other subscribers." Apple's iPhone and other new mobile products that deliver an array of video and DVD quality video will be commonplace. Technorati.com president Peter Hirshberg says "the audience wants to be the impresario, the conductor. The audience is in 'cahoots,'" which he laughingly described as "a technical term for when you build a

powerful global network that gives them power."
Hirshberg, recalling that computers were originally
referred to as giant brains, suggested "the giant
brain is us, and the power comes from people
gathering intelligence and control."

CHAPTER 9

VIRTUAL WORLDS:
REWIRING YOUR EMOTIONAL FUTURE

Forecasts for the future of human beings typically focus on bionics, genetics, drugs, therapeutic and behavioral rebalancing, mental and spiritual enlightenment, and physical enhancements. Neuro-sciences are all the vogue; there's an endless stream of books and articles on the relationship between the mind and physiological, psychological and sociological manifestations. A study conducted among Buddhist monks on the impact of meditation on brain matter has become a best selling book and was featured in a major *New York Times* article. Therapists, authors, gurus and guides ask us to get in touch with our emotions, but we're then asked to intellectualize our responses. We're told to get in touch with our heart and gut, but then instructed to *think* before we *act*.

The brain, heart and gut are, of course, integrated and connected. But we have authorized the brain to control our actions. Have you ever been ridiculed or reprimanded for being *too* emotional? Most of us have at least one time in our lives. Virtual Worlds are emotional outlets where expressing yourself is rewarded and where emotions, rather than intellect, define actions and relationships.

New generations born in the 21st Century will demote the brain from its position of dictatorial power over our emotional well-being. The emotional DNA of these new generations will evolve to empower the heart and the gut to manage and control actions and decisions with the advice of the brain but not necessarily its consent. This freedom from the brain's dominance and control compares to a fourth powerful force, the spirit, which also commands a higher position of authority over the psyche and intellect. The spirit has no physical organ to point to, but represents an all-powerful combination of the heart and gut that manifests in enlightened individuals and can take control of their feelings, decisions and actions. Virtual Worlds are appealing because they enable us to transcend our traditional existence and replicate a spiritual -- albeit not Godlike -- state.

Without engaging in medical (aka intellectual) debate over the power and rights of the brain, it's well documented that the average person utilizes only an estimated ten percent of the brain's functionality. Another ninety percent typically remains undeveloped. Could these under-used parts of the brain be centers that are intended to follow instructions from our heart, gut and spirit? Through an evolutionary process that empowers our feelings, could future generations open completely new powers of intuition, psychic abilities, mental telepathy and spiritual communications? By learning to elevate the emotions to a position of authority over the repressive forces of the brain, could we ultimately rewire our genetic code and activate powers that lie dormant and fallow in the brain?

In the next months and years, hundreds of Virtual Worlds will appear, offering us new opportunities to expand our relationships, our vision, our sensitivity and our ability to get in touch with our feelings about ourselves and others. We will become immersed in new situations and learn new ways to respond and react to these situations. Just as the population shifted from rural farm communities into cities and suburbs throughout the 20th Century, the growth of Virtual Worlds will be exponential over the next several years. Relationships among city-dwellers are very different than among residents of small communities. In that same context, relationships among Virtual World residents are dramatically different from the traditional relationships we experience in our day-to-day physical lives.

Virtual Worlds will change their inhabitants, just as the population of cities take on the characteristics of those cities. New cyber-civilizations are being built that will dramatically alter civilization itself. While change has been continuous, pervasive, and overwhelming, it has rarely been so dramatic that it totally alters the way people think, respond and act.

The rewiring of our emotional future has such powerful potential to alter the very nature of existence for new generations that virtual worlds will inevitably become more and more controversial. Forces will arise that will seek to control these cyber-universes, restrict the access of children, belittle their value and proclaim their danger to our youth and our personal freedoms.

These institutional forces need to be recognized for what they are: intellectual capital demanding to maintain its power over emotional will. This basic conflict has no victors; in its most simple form it is a generational evolution that can be slowed but not stopped. Future generations will look back at the creators of early Virtual Worlds in awe. They will look back at the technologies, systems, software and organizational structures of Second Life, Cyworld, MySpace and Gaia and marvel at how prehistoric they seem. There can be, unquestionably, legitimate criticisms of websites that capture people's time and attention for hours and hours. Parents especially will be appropriately concerned about how and where their children are spending their time and with whom they are interacting. Safety issues need to be at the forefront of controls over Virtual Worlds as they evolve. But the evolutionary advances that are the promise of Virtual Worlds offer hope for the future of human interaction.

Share your opinions on Virtual Worlds and their potential impact on humanity and relationships. Send your Virtual World stories to jm@jackmyers.com.

CHAPTER 10

CYBERPARADISESOCIETY.COM:

{A VIRTUAL WORLD
READER GENERATED FICTION}

The following fictional representation of a Virtual World environment will help you visualize life within a completely virtual existence. This first chapter of *CyberParadiseSociety.com: A Virtual World Reader Generated Fiction* paints a picture of an emerging mystery that involves the original creators of the most popular virtual world ever developed. It's the year 2030 and a female created and female-centric virtual society has suddenly embraced offensively male characteristics. Who -- or what computerized intrigue -- is behind the mystery?

These two chapters are just the beginning of our story. I invite you, our readers, to immerse yourselves in this virtual world. Send me your next chapter. I'll publish it, and then open it to our readers to write chapter 4 and so on. All accepted contributors will receive a share of the movie and future game rights.

I'll also continue to add free updates to *Rewiring Your Emotional Future*, so you can stay up to date on virtual worlds, their impact and influence. Subscribe by emailing Jack Myers at jm@jackmyers.com.

Www.CyberParadiseSociety.com

Visions From the Virtual Future

7:00 AM, September 15th 2030

Jenny's nightstand computer screen whirred to life and whispered "Wake up Jenny, it's 7 o'clock. You have to be at school." Jenny barely stirred. "Be quiet, it's Saturday," she mumbled. Jenny's virtual avatar, Ynnej*# processed Jenny's response and popped onto the screen. "Listen Jenny, you have a nine AM appointment with the department head to talk about your internship. You have to wake up now. And don't forget to take your vitamins."

Jenny swung out of bed and tumbled into the shower, quietly cursing that it was 'wash my hair' day and she hadn't thought ahead and washed it yesterday. Ynnej*# called out from the bedroom, "don't forget it's wash our hair day." Jenny smiled. Ynnej*# was her creation and it gave her pleasure when she tossed out clever reminders. Ynnej*# loved to get her own hair washed, and Jenny had promised Ynnej*# she could have her hair washed every time Jenny washed her own.

93

Ynnej*# was Jenny's best avatar yet. Since Jenny joined the CyberParadiseSociety 10 years earlier, she had created three versions of Ynnej, but Ynnej*# was Jenny's true alter ego. Jenny entered her own activities and calendar into her CyberParadiseSociety agenda; she programmed Ynnej*# with her own thoughts and emotions, creating a personalized, customized avatar who Jenny cared for almost better than she cared for herself.

Jenny won points when she treated Ynnej*# well; when she gave her a shampoo; when she fed her healthy food but with an occasional treat. She won points when she bought the brands the CyberParadiseSociety recommended, all of which were wholesome and bio-friendly.

Hundreds of millions of people around the world, mostly aged 20 to 40, of all races and religions, are active members of the CyberParadiseSociety.com in one form or another, with varying degrees of passion and involvement. The CyberParadiseSociety's impact on all aspects of global life is pervasive. It impacts culture, societies, and lifestyles. It contributes immensely to the success and failure of politicians, religious leaders, and virtually anyone who catches the attention of a CyberParadiseSociety crowd.

That meant almost anyone, so naturally CyberParadiseSociety both measures its members' passions and reports the passions its members embrace. The CyberParadiseSociety can make or break a new product, automobile, television show or celebrity. And, best of all, CyberParadiseSociety is a total democracy, with values and emotional connections determined by the majority, and with total freedom of the individual to manage his or her own world without infringement from government or institution.

Jenny created her own perfect virtual world in CyberParadiseSociety.com, and her latest avatar, Ynnej*#, was her representative in that virtual world and the virtual world's connection back to Jenny. Jenny loved Ynnej*# as much as she loved any human, maybe more. She cherished her avatar and spent hours every week devoted to Ynnej*# and CyberParadiseSociety.com participation.

But Jenny didn't have time to wash Ynnej*#'s hair this morning. She would wash her own, dress in her most conservative jeans and top, and head out to see the head of the *NYU Human Emotions and Non-Human Cultures Department* for her 9 AM meeting. Jenny was in line for her dream internship - a semester working at Global Paradise Games, the parent company that built itself into one of the ten largest companies in the world in less than 15 years thanks to CyberParadiseSociety, its first and still its most successful product.

Jenny knew she would win the internship over the hundreds of candidates. Her knowledge, love and passion for the virtual society gave her a competitive edge, plus she had all kinds of positive recommendations and perfect credentials. She aced the texts, breezed through the interviews, and now it was down to her and one other candidate, and their interviews this morning with the department head, Dan Wormer (yes, he's referred to as *Animal House's*

Dean Wormer both behind his back and to his face).
Both girls would impress Dan, but he was destined
to pick Jenny for the internship and he did. Her
passion, not to mention her subdued beauty and
perfect choice of tight Levi jeans and loose-fitting
knit non-designer sweater convinced him Jenny
would be a perfect match for the Global Paradise
Games corporate culture.

The company was created by several
computer geeks — all girls — at Syracuse University.
Winters there were cold (they used to be a lot
colder) and once the university brought Wi-Fi
networks onto campus for free high-speed access
anywhere, the girls began spending endless hours
creating the perfect world. The first nuance was that
this world maintained decidedly feminine and quietly
feminist overtones. Male passions and
aggressiveness were always toned down. Within two
years of its creation, every new movie was
premiered on CyberParadiseSociety.com and groups
would wirelessly connect their computers to large
screen TVs and gather synchronously to watch,
joining afterwards over virtual coffee (their

respective avatars actually got to drink the coffee) to discuss and debate the film, or just share gossip and stories about their day.

Of course, no one knew if the stories and gossip were true. Were they stories about the creator's real human experiences or made up fantasy lives? Most avatars have two lives at least, one with the avatars of owners' human friends and one fantasy life reserved for their virtual society friends. The creator always has the choice to introduce crossover experiences between physical and virtual worlds or avoid them altogether.

But Global Paradise's creators built into Cyber Paradise Society a unique twist on the rather typical virtual life social community it began as.

The unique twist in CyberParadiseSociety.com's design was the built-in conflict detection system that recognized dangerous interactions. Conversations among players weren't monitored, per se, but keywords and actions triggered an early warning system that caused closer attention to be paid by automated systems, and analyzed whether details being shared endangered any party to the interaction. This was the program code that catapulted CyberParadiseSociety.com and virtual worlds to legendary status and gave a small start up company founded by five students in Syracuse a global presence just 10 years later.

Jenny came home that Saturday feeling happier than she had ever felt in her life. From the subway heading back to her apartment, she IM'd Ynnej*: "we got the job. Start two weeks from this Monday at 10 AM. I'll be working in the Mind Events department as an event coordinator. We're in!"

At her end, Ynnej*# smiled.

Even though she was a human-like creature created and stored in a computer, she completely understood the implications of Jenny's success. For Ynnej*# knew that Jenny was on a mission to identify a group of CyberParadiseSociety.com players who were, Jenny was convinced, quietly rewriting the original female-centric manifesto sworn to by the original creators of CyberParadiseSociety.com. Jenny had noticed a definitive swing to a more male focus in the game playing, with car chases, extreme sports events, and overly generous rewards to those whose avatars participated in and viewed these male-centric events, along, of course, with their creators.

No matter how many Cyber Paradise Society members — and women were the clear majority of members — complained and no matter how many votes argued for a reversal of central policy back toward more female pursuits, the trend continued. By getting inside and working on the Mind Events team, Jenny was sure she would be one step closer to the mystery.

Actually, Jenny's job and her investigation were all part of the virtual experience. Hundreds of other players, as passionate and involved as Jenny, were packing their bags across the world to come to Global Paradise headquarters in New York for their welcome and initiation as the latest class of interns. Each was armed with slightly different information about the source of the swing to male dominance.

Most of the interns were women, but more than a third were men.

Each had empowered a group of friends, some they knew personally and others they knew only through their "relationships" in CyberParadiseSociety. These "friends" — actually avatars — were allies in the search to find the human source of the shift toward male dominance in the CyberParadiseSociety.com world.

The computers running CyberParadiseSociety.com and Global Paradise had long ago gained the innate intelligence to constantly create new challenges and opportunities for members. The swing to male dominance was one of them, but there were troubling indications the creators had lost control. Jenny and several other interns were convinced their mission was far more "real" than virtual. As Jenny prepped to begin her internship, there had been no indication of malevolence in the heart or mind of the CyberParadiseSociety.com computers, nor would there be for the seven more years the game would be in production before being closed down for declining involvement among new generations of Society members. Their disillusionment began that same first day Jenny began her internship job at Global Paradise. Jenny and the other interns, who were all joining the company to investigate the behind-the-scenes brain trust running Global Paradise, were about to send the CyberParadiseSociety cyber civilization into a tailspin it would not recover from.

On that same first day of Jenny's internship, not coincidentally, Gwen D'Allessio, one of the company's five original founders, was also beginning a new role. Gwen had remained with the company as chief developer and Jenny was her original avatar, a creation so real to Gwen that she often took on Jenny's personality and characteristics, and vice versa. Both Jenny and Ynnej*# were Gwen's creations... her avatars. In fact, all 100 of the interns starting their jobs were avatars, controlled by a spectrum of CyberParadiseSociety residents who had applied, on behalf of their avatars, for the position and had spent countless hours engaging in the competition to win a job. Gwen had never disclosed to her colleagues the identities of her own avatars, and by sending Jenny into the internship, she was hoping to uncover more than just the secrets to the pre-planned game that had elevated male roles to a more dominant place in the CyberParadise hierarchy.

Gwen personally controlled six different avatars in her CyberParadiseSociety world and she managed each avatar's world as a separate and independent virtual reality. Just as little girls' favorite dolls have their own little dolls and pets to play with in the imaginary worlds of their minds, CyberParadiseSociety.com was a layered world of avatars and their own avatar families.

Parts of Gwen's true "physical" personality filtered into each of the avatars. In fact, it was increasingly difficult to separate out Gwen's physical from her virtual life. She was equally invested in and dedicated to them all. Only occasionally did her own avatars interact with each other within the virtual world of CyberParadiseSociety. That would change in ways Gwen could not have imagined once Gwen's favorite avatar, Jenny, began her virtual internship at Global Paradise corporate headquarters and as Jenny and Gwen uncovered troubling changes in the corporate manifesto.

Gwen felt assured Jenny would represent her within corporate headquarters and that Jenny and Ynnej*# would continue to enjoy their role as Gwen's alter egos and personal support team. But she could not anticipate the role her avatars would have in the ultimate demise of CyberParadiseSociety.com and Global Paradise.

Gwen was convinced someone behind the scenes of Global Paradise was not only disrupting the fine balance of male/female relationships but was also using their access to personal records to play more than games. She sensed the cyber world she had created and loved was being altered in ways that could change the human virtual experience for decades to come. Were the changes to the operating DNA of CyberParadiseSociety the result of computer malfunction, or were humans the source of the disruption?

Gwen had personally met with each of the other founders, the Global paradise management team and the CyberParadiseSociety lead programmers. While they had intentionally elevated the role of males within the Society and all claimed to be committed to reversing the trend, all efforts had failed. Gwen and her colleagues had the inspired idea of inviting avatar interns into headquarters and giving them the mission of uncovering the cause of the programming changes and correcting them. Although Gwen and Jenny knew the problems ran deeper than the obvious, all other avatars still believed it was all part of the cyber game.

Of course, the other founders had also planted their avatars into the internship program, as had several of the management team and programmers themselves. They too wanted the inside track on discoveries and causes of the program changes at CyberParadiseSociety.

CyberParadiseSociety and Global Paradise Games are part of a fictional future that I'd like you to continue. Chapter by chapter, we will publish the rest of the story at www.CyberParadiseSociety.com. You're invited to share your ideas for Chapter 3 and future chapters by sending them to JM@jackmyers.com. Contributors will be fully recognized.

Jack Myers

Jack Myers is the editor and publisher of **Jack Myers Media Business Report** newsletter, considered a "daily first-read," by more than 25,000 media industry subscribers, and of MediaVillage.com, the online community for intelligent TV fans. He was identified as one of the "1,000 Most Creative Individuals in the U.S," is the recipient of the George Foster Peabody award for journalism, won the Crystal Heart Award from the Heartland Film Festival, and has been nominated for both an Academy and Emmy Award.

In the late 1970s and early 1980s, while a sales executive at CBS-TV, Jack co-created and managed the television industry's first integrated marketing sales group, and organized and directed the media industry's first multi-platform business development group. As a consultant from 1984 to 2000, Jack developed and recommended the business model for GM Mediaworks and Planworks for General Motors; advised Aegis Group on the business model for the launch of Carat Americas, and guided the sales, marketing, media buying and business development strategies for more than 100 media companies, agencies and advertisers. From 1994 to 1996, he conceived and co-developed a consortium of leading national advertisers to explore economic models for the development of advertiser-funded network television programming. Jack co-produced six primetime network television programs and the business models he designed have been implemented throughout the industry. In 1999, Jack led the first industry-wide Forums on Interactive Television Development, immersing him in new media technologies. Since 1984, his annual surveys of advertising executives on media sales organization performance have been the industry standards. The *Myers Emotional Connections Studies Defining the Engagement and Attentiveness of Audiences to the Media They Watch, Read and Use,* launched in 1999, have emerged as state-of-the art standards for measuring audiences' emotional connections with media, technology and advertising.

In 1995, Jack was asked by President Clinton to lead a delegation of advertising executives to the White House Conference on Children's Educational

Television. Jack is a Board Member of the Newhouse School of Communications at Syracuse University, serves on the Dean's Advisory Board for the Steinhardt School at New York University, is a member of the Academy of Television Arts & Sciences, and serves on the boards of several charitable organizations.

Jerry Weinstein

Only connect the prose and the passion, and both will
be exalted,
And human love will be seen at its height.
Live in fragments no longer.
Only connect...
 --E.M. Forster, Howards End

Forster's aphorism is Weinstein's credo.

Jerry Weinstein attended the Bronx HS of Science, which nurtured a life-long interest in the twining of the arts & sciences. A Harvard alum, he has matriculated in non-degree programs at MIT's Sloan School of Management and Harvard's Kennedy School of Government. After graduating from the Radcliffe Publishing Course, and receiving his MFA, Weinstein managed The MIT Press' Bradford Books, a founding imprint in cognitive science, where he published two of the Web's first online books, *Moths to the Flame* and *Noam Chomsky: A Life of Dissent*, and later consulted for Wesleyan University Press. Weinstein wrote the *Gay & Lesbian Alliance Against Defamation's* (GLAAD) bi-weekly newsletter, worked at Urban Box Office; and served as Senior Producer for LiveAdvice, which later became Yahoo! Answers. He has worked on a season of *Dream Job*, ESPN's foray into reality television, and is an instructor for barnesandnoble.com, where he has worked with authors including Augusten Burroughs, Michael Crichton, and Margaret Atwood. Weinstein contributes a weekly column to the *Jack Myers Media Business Report*, is the ghostwriter of *Handheld Usability* (Wiley) and has written several chapters in *The Real Time Enterprise*. Currently he is working on a feature screenplay about the largest extortion ring in U.S. history. Weinstein notes wryly that Forster's observation, "live in fragments no longer," failed to anticipate peer to peer networks, where fragments are the key to swift and sure distribution.

Order More Copies of Virtual Worlds™- Rewiring Your Emotional Future for $15.95 each

I want to order ☐ *copies of Virtual Worlds™- Rewiring Your Emotional Future*

Name
Title
Address
City   State
Zip
Phone   Fax
E-mail
☐ Credit Card   ☐ Bill Me
Signature
Fax to: 212-875-8023 or call: 212-875-8004

Or email Jack Myers at jm@jackmyers.com

Myers Publishing, LLC
125 W. 80th Street
New York, NY 10024
jm@jackmyers.com
Www.jackmyers.com
212-875-8004

Contents  2007.

Made in the USA